Wakefield Press

T0359666

Dark Bright Doors

Jill Jones won the Mary Gilmore Award for her first book
of poetry, *The Mask and the Jagged Star.* Her fourth book,
Screens, Jets, Heaven: New and Selected Poems, won the 2003
Kenneth Slessor Poetry Prize. Her work has been widely
published in Australia as well as in New Zealand, Canada,
the USA, Britain, France, the Czech Republic and India.
She currently teaches at the University of Adelaide.

By the Same Author

The Mask and the Jagged Star
Flagging Down Time
The Book of Possibilities
Screens, Jets, Heaven: New and Selected Poems
Struggle and Radiance: Ten Commentaries (chapbook)
Where the Sea Burns (chapbook)
Broken/Open
Fold Unfold (chapbook)
Speak Which (chapbook)

Dark Bright Doors
Jill Jones

Wakefield
Press

Wakefield Press
1 The Parade West
Kent Town
South Australia 5067
www.wakefieldpress.com.au

First published 2010
Copyright © Jill Jones, 2010

Cover designed by Liz Nicholson, designBITE
Text designed and typeset by Clinton Ellicott, Wakefield Press
Printed and bound by Hyde Park Press, Adelaide

National Library of Australia Cataloguing-in-Publication entry

Author: Jones, Jill, 1951– .
Title: Dark bright doors/Jill Jones.
ISBN: 978 1 86254 881 7 (pbk.).
Dewey Number: A821.3

For Annette

Contact
is
the art

Contents

Oh, Ground

What do I do
    without any legs
Walk on shadows
    simulacra

What's between my spine
    and my ankle
What propels
    the traverse

Even with my mouth
Even with
    the thought
    the cloud, the gasp
there is an
    evaporation

Ground – where
    are you, if
I step on you without feeling

Sorry I'm Late

The snow was in the sun
There was a prick in the garden
A truck jack-knifed the particulars
There was a smell of old gas
The crows lost
As did the roses and all that juice we spilled for love
That prick in the garden

Photographers were lighting bombs
The olive tree fell just as we were getting started
We forgot to fill out the form
Celebrity drug disasters were drifting in our channel
My watch shows tomorrow's date
The disk shattered
There's that smell again
It's a form of expediency, or is it complexity?

I tried to inform the authorities

If I could find my name and my reason
If the birds would stop drifting like that
If someone would lend a hand at the entrance
I'd be less nervous saying this
My throat would work with my head and hands

At Large

this is the handsome night
now unhidden from
salt and pepper days,
the east-west thickness
full of markets and cream,
all lit and stirring

but now, bypass the knife,
the gate, bypass yourself
into this night, limber, delicious
though you will never know,
even under a new torch,
how well dark it is

exhale, infiltrate, the 24 hour god,
in reconnaissance, growls
an original asking

Yeah, Yeah

Information is the mountain, yeah
and the mirror is the dark, brilliant.

Eyes are scratched as words fall in
tick, tick, tick – decision.

Blinking suns crack the ceiling
below is backwash, below, below.

Wired, weary in beautiful waste
then they turn off the air, yeah.

Story Board

1.
Versions of the classics, now flickering lights

About the menace of sabre tooth tigers
or what-have-you in the backyard

What matters – the grain
old concrete, stolen tusks

2.
Reaching across with paint through the hands

Pass the video camera, hang out a window
it's a car ride, a movie!

Division in the landscape
focus, not presence

3.
Influence of bees, bush flies or light

Here is no place – everything moves
written out of line – strokes, waves

Blended horizons drawn on the board
frame into frame

4.
The sadness in comfort, what all the words are about

The medicine show & tears
dust around airports

Switching voice away from the score sheet
even beyond the tent

5.
Resistance as a nostalgic process

Packing, unpacking
decision floating between noise

The arrows are pointing at the stars
amnesia spaces

Note:
Whatever you say goes on in your head.

Let's Get Lost

In a city of cameras and anonymous tips you must watch
the print-outs. There are toxins and steel at the axis.
Meanwhile, failed plans fall from belfries. Does all your
stuff seem like you? A set-up, over a woman? You can smell
fresh electrics from a dead hand.

But what about the enforcers? They have an aptitude for
chemistry and special alleys, they make toys for the new
avant-garde. Once they decide who made who, they bring
in the helicopters. Then it's time to trade up to a new
mission statement.

Maybe we can cut a deal even if we can no longer run the
presses. What if we say *no*, what if there were no files, no
history? Perhaps some good-old plastic surgery will give you
clean gothic lines. Or will you lie awake on your pillow
until dawn, rich with constructions?

We want kisses on skyscrapers, something visceral. Let's get
lost, like jokers, a pair of wicked stiffs.

Elsewhere

There are announcements in tunnels
across night. Somehow
you have to make sense of the lists
as they fall around you.

Across night, in the running
the corridors have called.
The lists want you to have them.
The lists are agitated
timed to the minute
as seconds disappear
past the spoken.
They un-recite clouds & feathers.

You notice them & ignore them
just the same
like your companions.
Distance used to be your guide.
Muscles worked in your throat
where you now swallow
some sour repeat pattern.
There was once a mystery
that train you've forgotten.
It rattled, now it glides.

You will be a line
in another announcement.
This is fame.

And the wind across corridors
blows night around.
You can feel its taste in directions.
There's still a rocking motion
even while you're waiting
to be late.
This is as close to salvation
as they can take you
to fair fields & water falls.

The dialogues are unwired.
They pass to sticky air
so quickly
handed around like chocolate
on the seat under spring sun
diffident in wind.
Packages crackle like leaves
the rain of stuff.

Pass it on, send it away
to the claustrophobic place
resting ground of ages
the cellophane light
the fidgetting bloody time.

This is the terror
nothing could be happening
all the time
as removed as it is on top of you.
Even gossip is pale now
a wiry thread that ignores duration.
You take up too much speed
this anxiety present.
You want to leap turnstyles.

And words that were lists
you've peeled them off like labels.
Only some of the glue
coats your skin less like memory.
You efface it between fingers
brush it away
on the cloth that covers you.
There's still that taste left
sweet old slick on your tongue.

This you can drink down
to make something in your body
its tunnels, its tenacity
hits on nerves.

But can you ever beat that game?
Do songs still come on
like pirouetting drugs?
Do corridors still fill up
excited & sprawling, shove & smoke?
Will you let the lists
keep you to your line?
Will you sing night, not say it?
Do you live elsewhere than
this scene?

The numbers are like rocks
chipped, dispersed
but still hard.
They're a trip-up, a deal gone wrong
the lie & truth told
on the fingers of one hand
but one is never one.
There's never one fire.

Regarding Pain

bodies
fall onto
their own shadows

does the jingle in
the air fresh solitude un-
settle the coming thought

shawl of rain
on street-brown buildings
no spare change

High Wind At Kekerengu

surf
talking infinities

gulls riding
what's left of the air

pacific turquoise

the pressure of the blast
takes the wing energy
to move in it

Esplanade Blues

Sometimes you're left with
things you never intended
to do – bush bashing,
mini golf, folk art –
or you're staring at the sea
past flax plants, the dark
sands, crayfish vans.
Out there albatross and orca
don't know what's coming
though in their way
they do, the never-ending
human tourism, with an eye
on paradise, sinking islands,
the lost valley, stealing
cedar and sex
and, yes, lands, oceans,
the very air, using
barques, canoes, black
panel vans of doof-doof,
extreme sports,
alpine symphonies.
Even the dog's bowl is made
from a paua shell.
Here's two cups of the best
organic coffee
because, boy, you're
going to need it
facing new year again
and the peaks, streaked
with dirty summer snow.

Sometimes you can be smiling
even if it's not what
you intended: 'you've got to
like what you do',
as the copyright expires
on classic cartoons,
so let's go nuts making T-shirts
with popeyed slogans,
eating our spinach,
enjoying the corrosive noise –
'do you hear the drums' – as tides
tumble grey and white pebbles
and bull kelp lies all around.
The salt gets in your head,
'the revolution never happened',
and what if it did,
only somebody wins.
Don't give up! Here's summer's
wisdom, a bottle of scotch,
a bag of weed, all bound for
bach-land. Here's a picnic table
by the memorial, another
roll of honour – everywhere
there's a list, seagulls
scramble the rest.

Waking Alone By the Radio

I am recovering from too much
drinking or dreaming.
You're phoning from up-country
with woes of a drowned camera
(corrosion, insurance and bruises).
Yet you can visit frozen cobwebs
around the verandah.

Morning radio trickles in its woes and strangers
a little piece of sky burnt bright
as it fell over Sydney this morning.
Listen to the astronomers explain!
Then there's the world
all the contusions we know and don't know
(my knee or my dream is stiff where it clipped the floor).

You tell me that down by the creek
there were twelve baby platypus, with bright eyes.
They are curious, you say
and no bigger than your hand.

The Thought Of an Autobiographical Poem
Troubles & Eludes Me

So I've been leaning against
the names of things
not just walls but the very air
the rug, the pen
the silver garbage bin.

But all words are
autobiographies
used to tell
half sentences
a quarter turning moon.

Today is a sound.
I hear words that mean
landing jet or rustled plastic
a book that depends on mercy.
And the gas, breathing.

Yellow Lilies

Day   by day   they are dying

as   day by   opening into yellow

into the stream   to fade   living

into the green   seen   through water

glass/lumen/split   the curve   falls

onto   an imaginary   and real table

Playing the Interim

I'm awake until morning with extremities and windows
then drowsy within your haven of questions.
The pattern on my dress has become a procession.
O road of noises and attractions, your dark bright door!
There are weeks when all poetries are night birds.
Your landscape is similar, the luminous dark entrance.
If I connect my noise too fast will it break like esprit,
its epithet a kiss upon the slow song's nerve?

Through the waste another wing moves above me.
I wake within a secret that once was a crime.
Better in the end to play the interim?
My bets were always slow little cowards.
I rub paint through my eyes, crisis in colour,
a medium of life, at last streams down my chin.
I continue opening the present rather than throw it inside.
Words to rain, my hair, your flocculent memory.

Envoi
If I close myself, nights become heavier,
uncertain as stars un-resisting gravity.

Insomniac Rhapsody Near Gilbert Street

You sleep in a little cage,
see the slats and bindings
of moonlight,
the glare of the Optus building.
Today another beer can
appears on a sill,
cars stop by for moments.
It's a characteristic of trade:
if you need the money
you need to relax and swallow.
It all ends up like an empty container
while the chains and the cherry picker
rattle morning, far too early
after the deal over the road,
the dog barking in the clinic
carpark.

Who says nothing happens here?
Each day mail is readdressed
and the police helicopter lifts
towards the hills.
On the radio farmers bless the rain.
Gouts of it drench the bitumen.
Another second is idling.
It's still months before the dust.
Somewhere – snow.

Something's melting in your brain.
Another dream
orgiastic as your old city
taking up the coast,
whose desalination
threatens your pH balance.
What runs through you will get you.
Sleep is only trash
you can't escape.

Oh, Sydney

What does autumn tell us
apart from the passing of seasons
and crows sitting on power lines
as trains weary their way in the slower mornings,
those mornings that aren't necessary
but cooler, while the news elects other avenues of feeling,
about devastation, which is difficult under the blue,
the azure feeling, when your clothes seem sharper,
tailored to crispness and to the needs of meetings,
all those people who think, somehow, there's something
    to say.
What is there to say, this breathlessness
won't uncover any other feeling than change
which you can breath as smoke, or a letter
that comes from another city you might like
to change into, but why, this place is more than enough,
its harbours and rivers, and the planes above,
constants in a changeable present, among
leaves and a daylight moon you could trace
in a drawing of your day, there's that rabbit's outline
on the surface of something other than the earth.
You make a story or a trace of it
but it only lasts while you look up, while along the street
you can't find a taxi or any way home that's without effort.

Argument sucks up the day hours and the night
should be free of this, but along the harbour walls
there is still doubt about who owes you the way
when here is millionaire's row, the swish,
the balconies full of none other than ourselves,
those selves with more money than we could pocket
though we dream, looking up, missing the light,
the vacant, the way out, past flyovers and factories
to a kind of ordinary, where the dog with three legs,
has wondered in the dog way, where a door might let out
onto the grass, for relief, and so near the river
once full of refuse, now almost desirable and making
a way past mangroves and mess to the bay
under flight paths and stars that have stared at the sea
but not quite in the smothered way the new century lends
to strands of time and night, and the call you make
not from a machine but a passion, that old call
you make from the restless body which somehow represents
the heart, the centuries, the wish and futures,
the faint smell of diesel, eucalypt, sandstone and tar.

Sedition

Music is the calm of a bracelet, girdle, helmet
inside words don't matter

I've found no terror in the package the song contains
there's a type of blue it resembles, one not grown ancient

the patina was freedom or something resembling
                                   the ability to finish the joke
they call for calm – you must give it up

standing on the platform with the sick trains
there are laws all around me

and the wind and the road, what of them?

Just Before the Curfew

noise
over head
this city cries

lateral
the road
lies down crushed

boom
boom ba-boom
the valley heaves

birds
hide in
the window shadows

come
let me
love you now

Excuses

The blue afternoon in stereo is more expansive in the
chorus, and the wing I imagine, a shadow the passageway
catches, voiced from trees, the gathering. On a map of
corners crisscrossed with falling there's a trace, my doubts
about gravity. The light was stolen from pages of prediction,
our hopeful meteorology, when you say the sails will dry.
And you are right as west wind peels the hour, the rows, the
veil that appeases.

Dust is busy at ground level.

I'm thirsty now as a motorcycle two-times the gutter among
spillage. All I can do is stand up once more. There's no exit
and the static is lively. This afternoon, however, concerns
nothing but the curve of the hill.

Skin Knowing

in the dark where skin
lights the way the rods
are perfect to hold on
to star pierce to leverage
the heights of, oh, this
small package je t'adore
just now in the know
even if you don't hardly
in the dark where skin

from this angle you are
all fuzzed the strokes
are kind and nothing is
on the level like a
drum skin fur erect
in the cold breath of my
finger topography hands
and over the swelling
from this angle you are

our hollow-bellied our
disported hands on our
down beat sings inside
there is no name
we do and we do and
undoing after our backs
turned our reflected hands
upturned the air
our hollow-bellied our

if this repetition do I
know you can we rise
above our gods and join
above our rise
and know if this is
skin
our
are

House Episodes

The sinews hold, bricks, braces, all superstructures where
stories hang, clown suits in the basement and wigs under
stairs. The hall is crowded with flowers and sleeping cats.
In the bathroom some punch-drunk visitor bows at the
basin full of pink tissue.

And who knows how the roof cavity sounds where all
summer we heard the scratching, red eyes of rats blinked
through the bed room ceiling. Later they ran into yards and
oblivion trails but they nested awhile above the other
episodes.

And there's still all this air, moving in the heat, body breath.

'Ae Fond Kiss'

What you make of my marks,
scratches on exercise books,
postcards advertising
zoos, surf boards, a hard luck story.

I've imprinted thick blue
coffee cups.
You can farewell me there
for the future's fond kiss.

In the next room
excavate vinyl rhythms,
crackling favourites,
love me do, please, love me.

If you can feel that warm
whorled thumb on the Princess Leia
toothbrush, waking you up
with a laugh-mint mouth.

Such things made us
happy, fridge magnets
in the shape of panda bears,
whales, memorised resin.

When you come upon me
if through dust,
hazed minutes, eons,
I know nothing as yet.

A dis-enchanted world
is truly frightening.
Play me
your song between tracks.

Seasonal Durance

At any end it's about Durance
& title – tho' calling a spade
A shovel near Xmas
Gets lost without party
Some years end in yellow
Some in smoky cumulus
This day is a slender Green
You can almost see the brush strokes

So holding on, like 'holding the man'
Is hard
But we are not men!
Which leaves us Outside, our arms
Lifting the minutes of the Rest
& holding our own green

Let's Taste

I've left my attitude, taken a slew of energy
The dope in me ducks, no more bitter

A familiar song: we shall never part
Remember the verb that got away

Forget your sex, taste then lips
Along my white shoulder, apparel falls away

Petals bruise my hand
after a wave of wild correspondences

No page entirely contains my wandering breath
Even the air is a strange grain

If you must, slip stealthily into the ventilator
Will the dollar be normal after that

But, wait, don't press my buttons, cast them aside
Let's shut up and dance

Mystery Train

The things you try
when you're 18
leaving nothing behind
so beautiful as 1956
a bell-hop's hat
ghost of a morning's love
in a river city
mysterious travellers
with, maybe, a .38
riding round all night
everyone looks like Elvis

Breath, the Hours

1.
what's in voices
streets, air's breadth, green on buildings
small glimmering gaps
between messages, scratches, if I had risen
once, ongoing after
the quiet, a fine strap of
sweat sighs and
unnerves the jokes, the flocking hours
each morning's expenses
slowly, exactly, moved far from lucent
cut to noon
awe is an engine, the particular
'*a glitch system*'
I am written in sky fresh
tunnels direct me
into the cool vibration of air
rain down does
as edges disappear, each stone on
the road, on
grey bright tears, distance in world
mortal affectionate hour

2.
windows silhouette scaffolds halfway up, into
gods among clouds
how the lights shine less lonely
while producing doubt
these shards are my parts of
form, empty again
becoming a reflection, birds hide in
the glass shadows
this brilliance shivers on us over
sound and smell
my lines and scales of skin
moving dimness there
to these hours, waste of revealing
savour in our
so common life, turbulent and fragmented
beginning of traffic
strives, fastens, inside skies, bright season
from what we
believe, they arrest you in passages
resist the wall
opened on me *this small lustrum*

3.

surrender moves me into long voice
hours blur lines
against open gates, threaded, poured, ached
gone and open
flocks seek me like air, from
my rare edges
after the weight of eleven dreams
the dog shadow
yes, white flowers live inside themselves
still as water
blue memory, prospect, and how to
complete change, rows
of voices, widths of water gleam
notches between messages
empty becomes still, petals hide shades
out of glass
draw long the shifted gates, look
the body which
mysteries penetrate! phase inside and always
the upheaval, edged
interlocks the black, night in markings

4.
if I had
the lifting! of wild flow rings
ruins to seek
an entrance which breathes the language
of mornings, 'it
seeks with me even then', working
remains, significances, each
step on the rise you resist
the way my
objections have glossed the going (old
arcades embrace, they
are glassy under clouds), experience is
a metaphor, if
it is the shape isolated from
qualm, parts of
a balustrade, 'sing to granulation, camber
hold it', piece
within the plot as draughts penetrate
the mobile darkness
doubt is an engine, the particular
wings its constructs

5.

rains not small
but blurred layers, season aspires to
favour so ordinary
life, words in writing me arrange
the sky, coolness
of any god, where it's possible
tactics resist ways
of language, burdens thirst, the pathway's
tongue, 'even sing
then I would', penetrate direction, the
pitch of ruptures
inside a quality of shade, centre
in a cloud
polisher of lights, *rained* one wing
climbs the chill
layer of fog startled that this
is peace and
skin with sun, morning's black beams
flower of falls
rain down does as hills disappear
hunger takes breath

6.

each day walks on terrain, crust
tasted in rock
curled, being born, turning with delicacy
once ongoing, after
the luminous grey distance, imaging shadow
hums of ashes
under vapour light still empties birds
breath spirit interlocks
the black way in the world
of the lip
in a sleep of clouds, blue
increase, asking – can
wild ruins go to their flowering
to refresh within
marks of rain, to fly night's
body of secrets
balance of apprehensions sketch long movement
(if you call
who answers) as resistance, your way
objection, however, leaves
edges and weft, risings, fields. observe

Elasticity

Whisper dry tracks,
veils, of ways
dream fuelled
like escapees.

I have my words,
their elasticity
connects skin,
the alive thought.

Magician!
The price of form.

The Green Dress

The desert erases regard, wind plays on.
A mirror looks back to the future which has no face.

I'm a player for the war outside.
My name has killed me, vaterland, vaster land, no escape.

Do not forsake me!
I've become the most beautiful green dress.

Maybe you would not recognise me
when the Johnnies come marching home.

You Can Only See

Pour the light into matter.
What remains, becomes.
You can only see.

Land folds along its lines.
Each space not the same as air.

What do you need to know
to walk it?

You can only see
land unfold
along the lines of its wounds.

The Tree Within

Here is the deep, cloud-catcher,
water in sky
where rapture drowns branches.

How we're marked by the dream
of colours, the interminable
and desperately beautiful.

Light comes and goes
not as flame but illumination,
prism of a place.

Your breath-part in air
depends on earth, not heaven,
the tree within and below.

'The sky ... a state of mind'.
Today it is 'exact and triumphant',
blaze of the white dark.

Sings Else

lights hang down yellow on yellow
loaded with contradictions rain starts falling
between derelict factories and slumbrous dark
winter wind
unsweetens
cold hands

all night long no particular tune
pretending to sleep still unopened rising
sudden tree smell from the book

looking for something you've thrown away
shape of a leaf a single
cricket nothing sings else out there
but shadow
going darkness
to water

Night Visitor

As if he means no harm, walking into the dream room,
childhood. He seems to know it, stepping between single
beds of memory, sure and faceless. I try to speak the
question or unveil the name in his absent eyes but at my
sound he vanishes, the stairs are silent, thin black air. One
night he stood still under the skylight, huge as a door, but
more often he's wandered the hallway or the foot of this
wider bed. He's called by a tight band beating, irregular,
across my ribs, hears my brain's low tide lapping the moon.
A year ago he was tall and thin, a sheaf of flowers clasped
heavy below his head. He reached down but couldn't touch
me. I lay there calling. For three days after he stalked the
semi-circle, refusing to leave the night. All he wanted was a
place for his flowers, a low place across my breath. Tonight
he's brought the past into my room, shuffled rhythms a
heart like mine hurries onto the only future sure to pass.
He's stepped between shadows, sure as solid, as winter
dark. If he speaks I'll vow to nothing, leaving the air open
for retrieval, sirens and the blood orange dawn.

But To Move

It's a straitened time for me, like
the era, parched, full of small agonies
related to bewilderment.
My pumice mind abrades its home,
there are no more arbors.

You hear each day alive in its runnels,
a kind of delirious mundanity that, sure,
can variegate at times.

You might need an up-to-date glossary,
or something shiny above the wall,
a wing off the sun, blithe in the way
it's taken you up again in ferment
of air, it's not pure but it moves.

By the River

sighing in mangroves
along with she-oaks

we speculate outside
with the wind

golf at midnight
on the islands

kids are tigers
slinging an iron

it's expensive living
on the ridge

To Montparnasse

We come on a train
in our foreign language.
We take paths, allées, passages.

We take hold of meanings,
ask their presence.
Tombs and bones dissolve.

To worry that light is dark.
The present becomes.

Sun swaps rain among hours,
washes meaning with colder matters.

We go away along Passage d'Enfer.
We make a wall.
We spread out memory.

Seeds

It's a concept that revolves
around flowers
that represents both the time
being and the time lost.

The future is all
that's present
in these other times
bloom and dust

a residue of carnation
rose and chlorophyll,
old worlds
remaking old worlds

here and now.

Listen, vases topple
and roots
become bone in the earth
that recycles us.

We are weeds and trees.
My petals fall
like seeds.

Cimetière Montparnasse

In All Directions

Winds change the road
matter opening
You laugh, in order to feel air
the bird of the thing

Blue crawls through the loess
You hope to escape
violent space, muddled air
collapsed topography
the end of output

Yet dark scripts escape
the interior animal, they
write to you from within designs
which tear through the whole

Load questions in the tongue's worm hole
Take a walk in all directions, write them

Evanescence

Surely weeds have rights
like cats' fur
    the feathers
at my front door
drops of
    evanescence
rain, dust
    the night's noise
It's not for nothing
    I might want
       to hide
from all these
pressing against
the curtain
    and it too
a little torn
    How did that happen
Who permits
    Who holds it
       close or apart
The chatter of
    machine

birds
welcome

All Night, All Night

Under erratic stars and sirens
raising us out of our beds,
the emergencies, the virus spreads,
how it ends, like a story,
who knows, through the grids,
through the planet's ways,
under the sway of the dark lit
with passages, the lake fills
far north, the planes bring in
more of those a-dying, we are
filled with facts, queries, nothing
so certain as each one's fear,
what will befall, what will all this
become, a plague of our making
or something we would rather not
done, but rise above the plain, ancient
in misery to find a place, divest
the hurt, who knows
what has ultimately been undone
under polypropylene, bad miming
of the original sung coasts, swarms
of blue fish, the white, the green,
the real schools so long
for the learning, underneath clouds,
but still, now, the sirens squealing,
and we must hurry along
in our caring, these bodies of ours,
kiss them while the world
is tearing, all night, tears all night
from the north and from the gulf
into here, past here, who will ask
where it comes from?

After a Zen Saying

The future glides in, big passenger wings
hopping down layers of cloud wash,
air space. In a carpark, way over, glass
fills with light as a gull turns above
bare trees and a memory of harbour salt
floats, the lilt of traffic, wash of
air conditioning tugs, and pitching phone talk,
the urge for walking into a blue sky afternoon
along the sea of coming and going.

The Wandering Poem

How words graph sky
and fall onto us. Fever dreams.
Doing, leaves, birds. This world.

The material empty lights through
in the running, still
or today, world of things.
Washed, curved.

Smiling in the haze, water moon.
Crows flying, white, dark.
The laughing unseen, under your feet.

To Overcome

it's well into night now
the district quiet
we must do what we can

clean our heads
before we settle for sleep
for we must be aware

as the noise in the quiet
will do what can
and not wait tomorrow

there's a conversation
out there with leaves
beyond policy

though the heart sinks
ground is still there
that and time

we'll do and we'll sleep
past the fallacy that
flight takes you somewhere

Getting Burned

'It's all gut stuff' he said or something like
she was 'afraid of the bunnies', or the crawlies, while
'the kinder are in the garden' with little stings and fun.
They're not paying attention, though somewhere else
is here too. The world isn't made of china
things crack, a crisis in the crystal. 'What is this
bombing madness' is no longer a question
and the yards not refuges are where you watch.
Come out to play, you will get splinters
you have not the stomach for but there is
more hunger than you understand, no longer
is there time for you if the plants won't grow.

You can say your finger was not on the trigger
the gun went off anyway.

The Round Earth

The vulnerable body bears a truthful fruit
(you can read too many books).
The first serendipity was a notion of paradise
somewhere on the up-side down where
shopping trolleys now encourage polymaths
and chinese whisperers understand the breath
of a different air. There's a future in curiosity
across the musical fence, predicaments, roots and routines

of travel raise a spectre of comparisons
and the dust of elsewhere. If you're building
a wall of books, leave the infrastructure
to the coconut palace, say 'I changed on return'
but the diagram of encounters always asks 'who do
we think we are?' – the faraway?

A Long Sky

broken breath spilled sky under fire's fluid
desirous space inarticulate clefts bone hair face
tipped into sunlight rust cooking impossible heat
endless world of summer beer voices power
lines beat of desert flares along trail

struck sore vaulted four-wheel beauty's sunset death
road kill have you heard it's a
long track that doesn't speak air vanishes
the idea is less solid we appear
in whips of melody cracks as gears
grind a caravan of song lake memory

mirage crouching at horizon comes gladly apart
in revenant wet

Dreaming Homeward

'Where shall there be an end of old and new'
         – Li Ho, *On and On For Ever*

Here are ten thousand changes, shading
sky and earth, along the river's mask.

What arrivals does it know
when all journeys dream homeward?

Is there a raft that can carry me?

I drift. Does it matter if I fail
under cloud spell?

I scrape light to its bones
keep guessing, water's true colours.

Each Side Of the Sky

The curtains are rocking,
so are the flies, circles
in motion, the wind
off the snow is rocking
the trees, sunset moves
each side of the sky,
daily, golden, clouding.

The trucks rock,
the cars, vans, kayaks,
the mind within
and without night-deep
dreaming, or morning's
bellbird – much to sleeping.

Wake! The sound
of fields and black beaches
rocking as seals
play the tides,
it's the moon's fault,
and the sun
making the sky blue.

The Between

We talk about beasts in winter
or breasts for months in heat
but today's ions rattle the hinges
and wings belly under wind.

Sleeky clouds, white pointers,
nothing holds when a sky streaks.
Wind eats up thought and spit.

Who Can Say When Her Time Is?

This is a song of the white.
The multitude or the pattern.
The rose or the wind.

A woman who begins,
a woman who disappears.
a woman drinking blossom's shadow.

There's a taste that becomes
with spring's movement,
its dreaming is intense. She knows

her secret virtue can be seen in
the water moon that must be (surely)
lying low, somewhere near.

Her body composes its treasures
beyond all the experts in confusion.
Her burdens lightly gather round –

the pure land or fever dreams,
plumes or rejected solutions,
the many-in-one or chaos.

She's never alone among memories.
What's supposed to occur now
is incidental to what happens.

Rising from the grass are fences
and clouds, those little brothers
playing games with the instant.

The moon takes its time.

My Satellite

The planets are marvellous tonight
and I would be with the new music

(*that was long ago, before
the new music*)

I'm waiting for power
like water, to shower upon my arms

I have some lifting to do

At the back door
grey moths are killing themselves
against the light

Are they crazy?
Perhaps it's the music

Summer has become
a deadly game again

My arms, what's
happened to my arms

if I'm too weak
to hold you up

Hey there, my little satellite
humming east into the change

each chord times
along with red planets
white and lonely suns

Angle Of the Sun

A yellow gleam bends walls open,
inside replenishes its fruit,
a quiet exhaling slips through day.

Breadth of flowers – welcome! extend!
Sun shapes the ordinary, an open drawer.
Hands perfect long silence and blue walls.

Or afternoon lateness raises light,
moves day weight, an instant circles
near motionless, books half hidden.

Intercept shape! catching as can.
Forms steep and soften, green, white
in the window's presence, brush flowers
as though they are slow, erasure

is never complete, curves are wild props
and what is collected, never still

Unfold

After cloud though not sudden
blue drops down the outside

voices slip and whisper rooms
heat rasps on structures

and the colours move to green
gold talks undersides of leaves

I feel myself crouching
in a new and awkward seat

unbalanced unregained

a heavy weight of summer
hard at windows

where is rain to separate us
from the metal force

pinned in a cold box
hidden from heat

(in skin water blood)
while duties tick on

I glimpse the shifts in sky

I should be wasting time

An Invention Of Laughter

Whatever I invent
has already become –
and gone.
The southerly outside
has its own language
which tears down certain
things – trees and stray breath.

There are no accidents.
The path is telling lies
rather than favours.
The Cross rises above
history's evening
and little children
droop like flags
in summer.

The water fills with sharks
smelling extinction.
Whose blood
swims the land?

Even if you were a bird
you wouldn't make it
against the blast.

We are uncovered.
The day goes metal.
Heat is laced in
the ice of the mind.
Shape changes shape
and walks across the Bridge.

The wolf lies down
with the wilderbeest
and rabbits cover the lawn.

Above us, the sulphur crest
laughter.

Nevertheless

Hear that stone in the mouth.
Of death within the other words.

Language uttered as bread.
The word for it is dust.

These Words

Once, you played around
in language.
It's still here, now you're gone.

Tell me it doesn't matter.
Or it's welcome as a faithless kiss,
tiring as history.

Every so often someone
comes by, rubs a finger
along your name.
Do you feel that now? Of course not.

The wind is strong, in winter,
in summer. All weathers
tear things up.

The traffic sings, it too is
on the move.
It will drive away.

Remember
these words?
World?
Away?

Material

Is it in the pattern of things
when the body's seated too long
there's no way to stand?
It's not even part of the pattern
as I look at my hand.

Thin or sticky – weigh the metaphors,
self telling self, tho' my fingers
tire at the root – the mass of leaves
over there, above steel lines,
they turn not quite like my palm,
the light silvery, in flashes, sublimations.

The arm swings, a pen runs out of itself
and a word seems spidery.
They are material and get used.
Now I think of hunger
and time on the watch bending again.

Figure

I'm sometimes very like me.
I can't get rid of the
poor little nonsense!

What can self do
with such visions?

Look at everything
with eyes
skirting the obscene.

Push on through
tearing the robe
exciting suspicions.

Always holding a little figure
something striking
very like me.

Broken Hour

I cracked it into ghost
sleep in a corridor
a broken hour

I had to slap up morning

a lame johnny that I
am I just disappearing
into the sweet grey

rain and rain and

anything the heart
touches rib roar
jostling a wing

dream on in-between

catching up with
the joke in the day
results leaders questions

what I cannot get

a grip or it stops
beating an old drum
dancing dissonance

its art as fatalist

O Fortuna

At times you're like a *machiavellista* planning to meet
whatever culminations you wish to thwart
on a Friday – well, it's nearly the weekend, the trees
are full of lorikeets and despite rain's desultory patter,
there's a fuzzy window of blue sky coming
from the south, wholly unexpected, the weather's
    governance
being a method above you. We all have our *fortuna*
we pretend we've never met, there's no point
in deception here unless it's your art. There's a timetable
dissembling just before the weekend, the doors of the end
carriage won't open as the train pulls up,
someone's limping under a backpack, you recall
your own blemishes. It's that 'tragic sense of life'
yukking around between faith and reason, the mortal
combat. While you work hard for the money, you want
to grab a towel and the 30+, hie yourself to the plage
dodging pale hooligans and melanoma. Surely
the end is nigh and it's a faith squeeze, when to be
heterodox, when to hold the line, which comes at you
up front and always, always leaves you past, belated,
but still humid with life at the turnstyles pushing
another weekly into the slot, watching it burst
up again. While folding your damp umbrella
into these sharp hectic hours, you keep appearing.

Notes/With Selves

self in weather
self with the owls
self that's gone away

arrangement of self
what doesn't self know yet
something intimate, something large

there's nothing in repose – even in the head
something on the level and
something unconscious

self and the hard men
self not bothering

selves with rain on their clothes
watching selves listen to music

rust and green tips, new gestures
the ongoing argument of selves
the tornado pen with words

self past murals – the flat otherworld
self and wet hair
self and creased newspaper

self and results
wet rails
keep self moving

the neverendingness
the push-me pull-you

tags and dangles, clasps
self arrives
and departs at angles

Leaving It To the Sky

I don't belong to generation green. I look out onto slate
tiles. Finally, there's rain on iron; piss-weak, though. The
phone falls so easily off the table. I don't believe in fake
tans, but I could. All around are little dogs. Hail, the queens
of suburbia! Every so often, it's the age of beige. Perhaps
you could win a sedan, be in business, not be a wanker. I
remember Friday's laughter down by the river. But the
swans aren't wild, just nasty. I'll never be a unit-shifter. I
can't explain why.

Wastage, control, a single low call rate. You can't be serious!
If you redefine The Problem That Has No Name, would we
be here at all? It's more than the mind-body poser. What
will make us think? No-one gets along in the news. I've
been on most of the rides. Am I my own provocateur? I
look upon the Westpac building and trace its sky tentacles.
This is an historic street with its geraniums, bottlebrush and
roses. And it's a windy Sunday; hear the bells of St
Somewhere in the city of quietude.

I'm thinking about my father's ukulele, lost things, the ink
patterns between east and west. Transcontinental!
Whichever way the weather moves, it's depending on blue.
I've never been relaxed and comfortable. Why does he yell
like that? All the space is above; over green iron, city plans,
the curve of sky is lost. I'm relying on radio, voices,
distance. All around, there's a smell of toast and tomatoes.
I'm having a yak with a piece of paper.

So, am I famous for not being famous? Do I lack an over-arching narrative? Leave that to the sky, give me Iced VoVos, cups of strong tea, and a work ethic. The smell of coffee says something. About me? Flesh imagines me back east, the desert imagines nothing I imagine.

A machine begins
noisy like all the machines
of our lives.
The rain that never was
has stopped.

Steering

my original air
after the storm
whose crow becomes
a small episode

coaxing my composure
and my insomnia
my nowhere sapphire
my rococo legend

rain, stone, cement
blonde on blonde
sky without formality
with morning brilliant

my ferneries and
thickets, my cover
is my silence
anything like yours

punching morning machines
hiding in letters
depending dust, wasting
too many problems

immersed as a
kind of solitude
dangling its allure
where, ever thankful

afternoons begin chantwise
cry first grit
and how sound
changes the heart's

music equal to
its night street
repertoire blurs lines
against my gates

electric dark extending
footsteps among secret
bones, voices spar
reverie loops float

dreaming I am
foam damps tomorrow's
wavelets, syllables dissolving
and revealing rocks

my fecund terraces
as openings stretch
from long voice
onto own shadows

the shifting ground
in the body
that brought no
conclusions with me

I am growing
into my hands

Acknowledgments

The following poems were first published, often in different forms, in the print and online journals, books and anthologies listed. My thanks go to the editors:

'Sorry I'm Late', in *Over There: Poems from Singapore and Australia*, eds John Kinsella & Alvin Pang, Ethos Books, Singapore, 2007; 'At Large', 'Yeah, Yeah', 'Material', 'Each Side of the Sky', in *nthposition* (UK); 'Story Board', in *Gut Cult* (USA); 'Let's Get Lost', in *Overland*; 'Elsewhere', in *Big Bridge* (USA); [shawl of rain], in *The Famous Reporter*; 'High Wind at Kekerengu', in *Otoliths*; 'Esplanade Blues', in *Blue Dog*; 'Waking Alone By the Radio', in *Space*; 'The Thought of an Autobiographical Poem Troubles & Eludes Me' in *Westerly*; 'Yellow Lilies', in *The Second Hay(na)ku Anthology*, eds Mark Young & Jean Vengua, Meritage/X-Pressed (USA/Finland); 'Playing the Interim', in *listenlight* (USA); 'Insomniac Rhapsody near Gilbert Street', in *Small City Tales of Strangeness and Beauty*, eds Gillian Britton & Stephen Lawrence, Wakefield Press, 2008; 'Oh Sydney', in *The Australian Literary Review*; 'Sedition', in *Cordite*; 'Just Before the Curfew', in *Babaylan Speaks* (USA); 'Excuses', in *hutt*; 'Skin Knowing', in *papertiger*; 'Ae Fond Kiss', in *Softblow* (Singapore); 'Breath, the Hours', in *The Drunken Boat* (USA); 'Elasticity', in *Poetryetc: Poems and Poets*, eds Andrew Burke & Candice Ward, Masthead, 2008; 'The Green Dress, 'You Can Only See', in *Fold Unfold*, Vagabond Press, 2005; 'Night Visitor', 'An Invention of Laughter', in *Divan*; 'After a Zen Saying', in *QLRS* (Singapore); 'Getting Burned', in *Moria* (USA); 'The Round Earth', in *Southerly*; 'Who Can Say When Her Time Is?', in *Eureka Street*; 'Angle of the Sun', in *Eureka Street*; 'Unfold', 'Steering', in *foam:e*; 'Broken Hour', in *Jacket*; 'O Fortuna', in *Heat*; 'Notes/With Selves', in *MiPoesias* (USA).

Some of these poems were first written for various projects with the DiVerse group of Sydney poets and read at exhibitions in Sydney galleries. Other poems were originally written for the *Poetryetc* snapshot project or for my weblog, Ruby Street.

'Waking Alone By the Radio' appeared in *The Best Australian Poems 2006* (Black Inc, ed Dorothy Porter), and *The Best Australian Poetry 2007* (UQP, ed John Tranter). 'The Thought of an Autobiographical Poem Troubles & Eludes Me' appeared in *The Best Australian Poetry 2008* (UQP, ed David Brooks). 'Oh Sydney', appeared in *The Best Australian Poems 2009*, (Black Inc, ed Robert Adamson).

Notes

'Mystery Train' refers to scenes in the Jim Jarmusch film of the same name.

'The Green Dress', after 'Snow White Joins Up' by Klaus Friedeberger.

'You Can Only See', after 'You Yangs Landscape' by Fred Williams. Includes a phrase based on a line in Heraclitus as used in Denise Riley's *The Words of Selves*.

'The Tree Within', after 'Lagoon, Wimmera' by Sidney Nolan. Quotes from a letter written by Sidney Nolan to Cynthia Nolan, 24 February 1964.

'Dreaming Homeward', after 'Riverbend' by Sidney Nolan.

'Who Can Say When Her Time Is?', after 'Rosa Mutabilis' by Sidney Nolan.

'Angle of the Sun', after 'Chinese Screen and Yellow Room' by Margaret Olley.

Wakefield Press is an independent publishing and
distribution company based in Adelaide, South Australia.
We love good stories and publish beautiful books.
To see our full range of titles, please visit our website at
www.wakefieldpress.com.au.